ELIZABETH PACKARD:

Breaking Chains of Silence and Oppression

NELSON S. SOLOMON

Copyright©2023 Nelson S. Solomon

All rights Reserved

TABLE OF CONTENT

INTRODUCTION 5

CHAPTER ONE 7
- EARLY LIFE AND BACKGROUND 7
  - Education and Early Influences 8

CHAPTER TWO 11
- MARRIAGE AND MOTHERHOOD 11
  - Marriage to Theophilus Packard 11
  - Life as Wife and Mother 12

CHAPTER THREE 15
- THE JOURNEY TO ADVOCACY: BREAKING THE CHAINS OF CONVENTION 15
  - Awakening to the Women's Rights Movement 15
  - Elizabeth's Initial Involvement 17

CHAPTER FOUR 19
- CHALLENGING THE ASYLUM SYSTEM: A DESCENT INTO DARKNESS. 19
  - The Tragic Decision to Institutionalize Elizabeth 19

CHAPTER FIVE 25
- WRITING HER WAY TO FREEDOM: THE PEN AS A MIGHTY SWORD ... 25
  - Elizabeth's Writings and Publications 25
  - The Impact of Her Books and Essays 27

CHAPTER SIX 29
- LEGAL BATTLES AND ACTIVISM: A BATTLE CRY FOR JUSTICE 29
  - Elizabeth's Fight for Her Freedom 29
  - Advocating for the Rights of Institutionalized Women 31

CHAPTER SEVEN 35
- LEGACY AND IMPACT: A TRAILBLAZER'S ENDURING INFLUENCE 35
  - The Lasting Influence of Elizabeth Packard 35

Her Contribution to the Women's Rights Movement........................*37*
CHAPTER EIGHT **41**
    LATER LIFE AND DEATH...41
CONCLUSION **43**

INTRODUCTION

In the midst of the 19th-century, an era defined by societal norms and expectations, a remarkable woman emerged from the shadows. Her name was **"Elizabeth Packard"**, and her story is a testament to resilience and the indomitable spirit of those who dared to challenge the status quo.

Amidst the corsets, horse-drawn carriages, and a world dominated by male authority, Elizabeth's life unfurled like an unwritten chapter in the annals of history. As you delve into this biography, you will journey through a time when women's voices were often stifled, their aspirations overlooked, and their individuality suppressed.

But Elizabeth Packard was no ordinary woman. She defied convention, questioned the unquestionable, and transformed her own plight into a rallying cry for countless others. Her tale is one of courage and conviction, a story that will grip your heart and stir your soul.

Prepare to be captivated by the intricacies of a life marked by adversity and injustice, as we follow Elizabeth's path from a seemingly ordinary existence to becoming a symbol of unyielding determination. Her journey is a poignant reminder that the power to break free from silence and oppression resides within each of us. This biography unveils the extraordinary life of Elizabeth Packard, a woman who not only shaped her own destiny but also left an indelible mark on the struggle for women's rights and mental health reform. As you turn the pages, you'll witness a portrait of strength, a narrative of change, and an inspirational tale that will leave you yearning for more.

CHAPTER ONE

Early Life and Background

In the quiet town of Ware, Massachusetts, on the 28th of December, 1816, a seed of change was sown in the form of a baby girl. Elizabeth Parsons Ware was born into a world vastly different from the one we know today, a world where the rights and roles of women were rigidly defined. Her early life and the formative years of her education were, in many ways, the soil from which her unyielding spirit would later bloom.

Elizabeth was the second of three children born to Lucy Parsons Ware and Asa Ware, a minister in the Congregational Church. Her father's role as a clergyman meant that the Ware household was deeply entrenched in the religious and moral values of the time. As the young Elizabeth grew, she was exposed to the strong convictions and beliefs of her father, which played a significant role in shaping her character. As a child, Elizabeth was known for her inquisitive mind and an unquenchable thirst for knowledge. Her early years were marked by a sense of curiosity that set her apart from her peers. She was not content with merely accepting the norms and expectations placed upon women of her era; she yearned for a deeper understanding of the world around her.

It is important to note that the Ware family's life was far from the struggles and hardships that would later come to define Elizabeth's own existence. In her early years, she enjoyed the comfort and security of a loving family, which provided her with a stable foundation from which she could embark on her transformative journey.

Education and Early Influences

Elizabeth's education, during her formative years, was an exceptional privilege, considering the limited opportunities available to women at the time. She attended Ipswich Female Seminary, where she received an education that far exceeded the basic knowledge typically afforded to young women of her era. The Ipswich Female Seminary, founded by Zilpah Grant and Mary Lyon, was a pioneering institution in providing advanced education to young women. It was here that Elizabeth was introduced to subjects that were considered unconventional for women, such as literature, history, and philosophy. These early influences, coupled with her father's teachings, kindled a passion for intellectual pursuits that would shape the course of her life.

As Elizabeth grew and continued her education, her evolving views and beliefs began to diverge from the conservative doctrines of her father's faith. She found herself drawn to the burgeoning women's rights movement and began to question the prevailing norms of her society. The seeds of rebellion were sown during her early years of education, and they would sprout into a steadfast commitment to challenging the status quo.

It's worth noting that Elizabeth's early life and education were a sanctuary of intellectual freedom compared to the oppressive constraints that awaited her in her later years. Her experiences during this time laid the foundation for her future endeavors and her unwavering commitment to the rights of women.

CHAPTER TWO

Marriage and Motherhood

Marriage to Theophilus Packard

In the early 19th century, marriage was often considered the ultimate aspiration for women, the doorway to respectability and security. Elizabeth's life followed a path that was typical for women of her time, yet it would soon take a divergent and challenging turn.

At the age of 24, Elizabeth married Theophilus Packard, a Presbyterian minister, in 1841. Theophilus was a man of strong religious convictions, and their union was rooted in their shared faith. On the surface, it appeared to be a conventional match, but the dynamics within their marriage would prove to be far from ordinary.

Theophilus, a man who staunchly adhered to the traditional gender roles of the era, saw himself as the head of the household. His interpretation of marriage was firmly entrenched in the belief that a woman's role was to be submissive to her husband. As such,

Elizabeth found herself thrust into a marriage that mirrored the prevailing norms of the time, where a wife's duty was to obey and support her husband's endeavors.

Life as Wife and Mother

Elizabeth's role as a wife and mother was largely shaped by the societal expectations of the 19th century. The Packards settled in Manteno, Illinois, where Theophilus served as a minister. Elizabeth, in accordance with the prescribed roles for women, took on the responsibilities of a homemaker and mother. She bore her husband four children during the early years of their marriage, which further cemented her place in the domestic sphere.

The demands of motherhood and homemaking were all-consuming, as she tended to the needs of her growing family. Her life revolved around the care of her children, the management of their home, and her husband's ministry. Elizabeth's days were filled with the relentless duties of child-rearing and maintaining a household, all of which conformed to the conventional expectations of a wife in the 19th century.

However, even in the confines of her domestic role, Elizabeth's intellectual curiosity and independent spirit persisted. Her early education and exposure to unconventional ideas continued to influence her perspective on the world, and she was not content to be merely a passive participant in her own life.

As the years passed, the traditional roles of wife and mother became increasingly restrictive for Elizabeth. Her growing awareness of the limitations placed on women during this era ignited a spark within her, one that would eventually lead to her questioning the authority of her husband and the oppressive nature of her marriage.

Elizabeth's experiences as a wife and mother would play a pivotal role in shaping her future advocacy. Her transformation from a conforming wife to a determined advocate for women's rights and mental health reform was a process that unfolded over time, influenced by the societal constraints she encountered within the framework of her marriage and the confines of motherhood.

CHAPTER THREE

The Journey to Advocacy: Breaking the Chains of Convention

Awakening to the Women's Rights Movement

The mid-19th century was a period of profound social change and upheaval, with movements for reform and equality gaining momentum. Women's voices, which had long been stifled, began to resonate with calls for justice, equality, and recognition. It was within this dynamic and transformative context that Elizabeth Packard, once bound by the traditional roles of wife and mother, found her voice and a new sense of purpose.

Elizabeth's awakening to the women's rights movement was a gradual process, sparked by her growing awareness of the inequities and injustices faced by women in her time. Her early exposure to the intellectual currents of the Ipswich Female Seminary, where she had received an education that far exceeded the norms for women, had planted the seeds of independent thought. These seeds sprouted into a deep-rooted conviction that women deserved a greater role in society.

The year 1848 marked a turning point in the women's rights movement with the Seneca Falls Convention, where the famous Declaration of Sentiments was adopted. This historic event, which Elizabeth would later look back upon with great significance, sought to address the social, economic, and political inequalities faced by women. It was a clarion call for the recognition of women's rights and a demand for equality with men.

Elizabeth, however, was not an immediate participant in the women's rights movement. Her initial involvement was indirect, driven by her voracious appetite for reading and the exchange of ideas. The Packard household was filled with books, and Elizabeth devoured a wide range of literature, including the works of prominent feminists and social reformers of the time. Her growing familiarity with the writings of women's rights advocates such as Elizabeth Cady Stanton and Lucretia Mott ignited a spark within her.

Her burgeoning interest in the movement was further fueled by her own experiences as a woman within the constraints of her marriage. The stifling expectations placed upon her as a wife and mother, the lack of autonomy and the sense of subjugation, all stirred within her a longing for change. She began to see parallels between her own life and the struggles faced by women across the nation.

Elizabeth's Initial Involvement

Elizabeth's journey into the women's rights movement took a more active turn when she encountered the writings of famous women's rights activists, such as Susan B. Anthony and Lucy Stone. Their words resonated deeply with her, as they articulated the frustrations and aspirations she had long held in her heart.

It was in her secret moments of reading and reflection that Elizabeth first contemplated the possibility of women's rights advocacy. She yearned to contribute to the cause, to lend her voice to the chorus of change. However, the prospect of engaging in public activism was fraught with challenges, given the constraints imposed upon her as a married woman.

Nonetheless, Elizabeth began to correspond with and support the efforts of prominent women's rights advocates, including Susan B. Anthony. These letters and exchanges, though initially private, marked her early involvement in the movement. She found a sense of solidarity and encouragement from her interactions with women who, like her, sought to dismantle the chains that bound them.

Elizabeth's growing commitment to the women's rights movement coincided with her own personal transformation. She was shedding the cloak of convention that had defined her earlier years as a wife and mother. Her awareness and convictions were evolving, and she began to see herself not only as an individual but as a woman who could effect change.

CHAPTER FOUR

Challenging the Asylum System: A Descent into Darkness

The Tragic Decision to Institutionalize Elizabeth

The 19th century was a time when society's perception of mental illness was shrouded in misconceptions and ignorance. It was an era when individuals who displayed unconventional behavior or held opinions deemed contrary to the societal norm were often labeled as "insane" and subjected to a horrifying fate. This was the grim backdrop against which Elizabeth Packard, an unconventional thinker who dared to challenge societal conventions, found herself ensnared.

The decision to institutionalize Elizabeth Packard was a tragic turning point in her life, and it was a decision made by none other than her husband, Theophilus Packard. Theophilus, a staunch advocate for traditional gender roles and a rigid believer in the authority of husbands over their wives, saw Elizabeth's evolving views on women's rights and religion as a threat to his authority and the stability of their household.

In the eyes of Theophilus, Elizabeth's outspokenness and her increasing independence marked her as mentally unstable. Her steadfast commitment to the women's rights movement and her growing assertiveness challenged his sense of control. To him, her behavior was not only unconventional but also dangerous. In a shocking and deeply distressing move, he sought the legal means to have his wife declared insane and committed to an asylum.

The court proceedings that followed were a harrowing ordeal for Elizabeth. Her husband, armed with the authority granted to him by the prevailing laws of the time, argued that her beliefs and actions were indicative of insanity. Elizabeth, on the other hand, vehemently defended her sanity and articulated her commitment to the cause of women's rights. It was a battle between two opposing worldviews, one that epitomized the societal conflict of the era.

The court's ruling, unsurprisingly, favored Theophilus. In a verdict that reflected the deeply entrenched gender biases of the time,

Elizabeth Packard was declared insane and committed to the Jacksonville Insane Asylum. This decision marked the beginning of a nightmarish chapter in her life, one in which she would face unimaginable hardships and injustices.

Her Ordeal in the Jacksonville Insane Asylum

The Jacksonville Insane Asylum, where Elizabeth was confined, was a grim and foreboding institution. It was a place where the mentally ill, the socially nonconforming, and those who dared to challenge the established order were subjected to conditions that can only be described as dehumanizing.

Upon her arrival at the asylum, Elizabeth was stripped of her identity and autonomy. She was separated from her children, deprived of her personal belongings, and subjected to a regimen of treatment that included isolation, restraints, and the administration of harsh drugs. The conditions within the asylum were inhumane, with overcrowded and unsanitary quarters that offered no respite for its inmates.

Elizabeth's time in the asylum was marked by isolation, abuse, and the relentless efforts of the institution's staff to break her spirit. However, she refused to succumb to the dehumanizing treatment to which she was subjected. She maintained her sanity and a tenacious resolve to challenge the unjust confinement imposed upon her.

During her time in the asylum, Elizabeth's mental fortitude remained unshaken. She managed to communicate with the outside world, secretly writing letters to family and friends that detailed her plight and her steadfast commitment to the cause of women's rights. These letters would later become a vital lifeline, shedding light on the horrors within the asylum and drawing attention to the need for reform.

The ordeal Elizabeth endured within the Jacksonville Insane Asylum was a testament to her resilience and her unyielding spirit. It was a time of suffering, but it also became a period of profound transformation. Elizabeth's experiences within the walls of the asylum would ultimately propel her into a new and unexpected role as a fearless advocate for the rights of institutionalized women.

CHAPTER FIVE

Writing Her Way to Freedom: The Pen as a Mighty Sword

Elizabeth's Writings and Publications

The Jacksonville Insane Asylum, where Elizabeth Packard was unjustly confined, was a place of despair and darkness. Yet, within the walls of this institution, a glimmer of hope emerged, fueled by Elizabeth's unwavering determination to challenge the status quo and bring about change. Her weapon of choice in this struggle was the written word, and her writings and publications would become a powerful force for her own liberation and the liberation of countless others.

In the early days of her confinement, Elizabeth found herself isolated from her children, her home, and the world she had known. Her rights had been stripped away, and she was subjected to the oppressive authority of the asylum staff. However, her spirit remained unbroken, and she turned to writing as a means of maintaining her sanity and asserting her identity.

Elizabeth began to document her experiences within the asylum, chronicling the injustices, abuses, and the deplorable conditions she witnessed. These writings served not only as a lifeline to the outside world but as a testament to her own sanity and the injustice of her confinement. Her words were a declaration of her resistance to the arbitrary power that had placed her in the asylum.

The impact of Elizabeth's writings extended beyond the walls of her confinement. She clandestinely wrote letters to family and friends, sharing her experiences and her commitment to the cause of women's rights. Her letters were a cry for help, a call to action, and a defiant assertion of her own humanity.

Her advocacy extended to her writings within the asylum. Elizabeth composed essays that challenged the prevailing notions of insanity and the treatment of women who had been labeled as such. Her essays were a courageous critique of the asylum system and a call for reform. She argued passionately for the rights of institutionalized women and the need for a more humane approach to their care.

The Impact of Her Books and Essays

Elizabeth's writings were not confined to the pages of her journal or her letters. They became the foundation of her first book, "Three Years in a Mad-House." This publication, which chronicled her experiences in the Jacksonville Insane Asylum, was a groundbreaking exposé of the conditions within such institutions and the unjust confinement of women.

"Three Years in a Mad-House" sent shockwaves through society. It was a searing indictment of the asylum system, revealing the horrors that had been concealed behind closed doors. Elizabeth's firsthand accounts of abuse, neglect, and the denial of basic human rights struck a chord with readers and activists of the time.

The book not only drew attention to the injustices within asylums but also challenged the prevailing societal attitudes toward women. It called for a reevaluation of the criteria used to label women as insane, recognizing that many were institutionalized not due to mental illness but as a means of control and suppression.

Elizabeth's writings and her advocacy within the asylum led to a groundswell of support for her cause. She received countless letters from individuals who were moved by her story and eager to support her efforts. Her own family, once torn by the conflict surrounding her confinement, rallied to her side.

The impact of her work extended to the legal sphere as well. Elizabeth's writings were instrumental in a series of court battles to secure her release from the asylum. These legal proceedings challenged the authority of husbands over their wives and the unjust confinement of women. In a historic decision, the Illinois Supreme Court ruled in her favor, declaring that she had been unjustly deprived of her liberty.

The publication of "Three Years in a Mad-House" and the subsequent legal victories not only secured Elizabeth's own freedom but also marked a significant turning point in the treatment of institutionalized women and the perception of women's rights in the 19th century.

CHAPTER SIX

Legal Battles and Activism: A Battle Cry for Justice

Elizabeth's Fight for Her Freedom

The story of Elizabeth Packard's life is a testament to resilience and the unwavering pursuit of justice. Her unjust confinement within the Jacksonville Insane Asylum was a nightmare that seemed to have no end, but she was determined to break free from her chains and assert her rightful place in the world. Her path to freedom was paved with legal battles, activism, and an unyielding commitment to challenging the status quo.

Upon her commitment to the asylum, Elizabeth was thrust into a legal battle that would not only define her life but also shape the course of women's rights and mental health reform in the 19th century. She refused to accept the court's verdict that had declared her insane and confined her against her will. In her eyes, the injustice was clear, and she was determined to overturn the decision that had deprived her of her liberty.

Her legal journey was marked by tenacity and unwavering faith in the principles of justice. She challenged the authority of her husband, Theophilus Packard, who had orchestrated her commitment to the asylum. In a society where the law favored the control of husbands over their wives, Elizabeth's pursuit of justice was a daring act of rebellion. She was not only fighting for her own freedom but also for the recognition of women as individuals with rights independent of their husbands.

Elizabeth's legal battles were fraught with challenges and obstacles. She faced opposition from her husband, societal norms that favored male authority, and a legal system that was biased against women. Her case went through several rounds of legal proceedings, each marked by fierce determination and passionate advocacy for her own cause and the broader cause of women's rights.

The turning point came when the Illinois Supreme Court, in a historic decision, ruled in her favor. The court's decision not only secured her release from the asylum but also set a precedent that would impact the legal status of married women and the authority of husbands in the state. It was a landmark victory for women's rights and a testament to Elizabeth's unyielding commitment to justice.

Advocating for the Rights of Institutionalized Women

Elizabeth's legal victory was not the end of her journey; it was only the beginning. Her experiences within the Jacksonville Insane Asylum had exposed her to the horrors of institutionalization and the injustices faced by women labeled as insane. It was a revelation that compelled her to become a voice for those who remained confined and voiceless.

Upon her release, Elizabeth embarked on a mission to advocate for the rights of institutionalized women. She was driven by a deep sense of empathy and a determination to expose the abuses and mistreatment that had been concealed within asylums. Her advocacy was rooted in her firsthand knowledge of the deplorable conditions and the arbitrary confinement that many women endured.

Elizabeth became a prolific writer and speaker, using her platform to shed light on the plight of institutionalized women. She traveled across the country, sharing her own experiences and advocating for reforms in the treatment of the mentally ill. Her speeches and writings served as a rallying cry for change and a call to society to recognize the humanity and rights of those who had been confined.

One of her notable contributions was the establishment of the Anti-Insane Asylum Society, an organization dedicated to advocating for the rights of institutionalized women. Through this organization, Elizabeth worked tirelessly to expose the abuses within asylums and to push for legislative changes that would safeguard the rights and dignity of the mentally ill.

Her work extended to the realm of legislative reform. Elizabeth was instrumental in influencing changes to the laws regarding the commitment of individuals to asylums. Her tireless efforts contributed to reforms that aimed to prevent arbitrary institutionalization and to provide safeguards for the rights of those within asylums.

Elizabeth's activism and advocacy were not limited to mental health reform; they were also intertwined with the broader women's rights movement of the 19th century. Her experiences as a woman who had been silenced and confined served as a powerful reminder of the injustices faced by women in a society that often denied them a voice.

CHAPTER SEVEN

Legacy and Impact: A Trailblazer's Enduring Influence

The Lasting Influence of Elizabeth Packard

The legacy of Elizabeth Packard is one that reverberates through the annals of women's history, mental health advocacy, and the broader struggle for justice and equality. Her life, marked by adversity and unwavering determination, left an indelible imprint on the world, and her influence continues to resonate in the fight for human rights.

Elizabeth's enduring influence can be traced through several facets of her remarkable life:

Women's Rights Advocacy

Elizabeth Packard's advocacy for women's rights was not confined to her era. Her courageous stand against the prevailing norms of her time, her legal battles for her own freedom, and her vocal condemnation of the institutionalization of women marked her as an early pioneer in the women's rights movement. Her determination to challenge the authority of husbands over their wives and to assert women's independence as individuals with rights set a precedent for the evolving landscape of gender equality.

Mental Health Reform

Elizabeth's experiences within the Jacksonville Insane Asylum and her subsequent activism cast a spotlight on the dire need for reform in the treatment of the mentally ill. Her efforts to expose the abuses and mistreatment of institutionalized women led to legislative changes aimed at safeguarding the rights and dignity of those confined to asylums. Her work within the Anti-Insane Asylum Society and her commitment to improving the lives of the mentally ill remain a testament to her enduring impact on mental health advocacy.

The Power of the Pen

Elizabeth Packard's writings, including her book "Three Years in a Mad-House," were instrumental in exposing the horrors within asylums and the injustices faced by institutionalized women. Her written words served as a rallying cry for change, drawing attention to the need for reform and challenging societal norms. Her success in using the written word as a tool for advocacy demonstrates the transformative power of literature and the importance of sharing one's experiences to effect change.

Inspiration for Generations

Elizabeth's story has served as an enduring source of inspiration for generations of women and advocates for justice. Her resilience in the face of adversity, her unwavering commitment to her principles, and her ability to challenge the status quo have made her a symbol of courage and determination. Her legacy continues to inspire individuals who face discrimination, confinement, or oppression to find their voice and stand up for their rights.

Her Contribution to the Women's Rights Movement

Elizabeth Packard's contribution to the women's rights movement was both profound and multifaceted. As a pioneering figure in the 19th-century struggle for women's rights, her influence extended through the following key areas:

Challenging Gender Norms

Elizabeth's refusal to accept the limitations imposed upon her as a wife and mother challenged the prevailing gender norms of her time. Her assertion of her independence and her involvement in the women's rights movement were acts of rebellion against a society that sought to silence and confine women to domestic roles.

Legal Precedent

Through her legal battles to secure her own freedom, Elizabeth Packard set a legal precedent that contributed to changing the legal status of married women. The Illinois Supreme Court's ruling in her favor acknowledged the right of women to assert their independence and challenged the authority of husbands over their wives.

Advocating for Institutionalized Women

Elizabeth's advocacy extended to the rights of institutionalized women, a group that had long been voiceless and oppressed. Her work within the Anti-Insane Asylum Society and her exposure of abuses within asylums contributed to the broader conversation about the treatment of the mentally ill and the need for reform.

Inspiration for Suffragists

Elizabeth Packard's determination and activism inspired suffragists and women's rights advocates of her time, including prominent figures like Susan B. Anthony and Elizabeth Cady Stanton. Her story served as a rallying point for women who sought to challenge societal constraints and assert their rights.

Elizabeth Packard's life and contributions to the women's rights movement represent a foundational chapter in the ongoing struggle for gender equality. Her unwavering commitment to justice and her courage in the face of adversity serve as an enduring reminder that the fight for women's rights is a journey marked by individuals who refuse to be silenced and who blaze a trail for future generations.

CHAPTER EIGHT

Later Life and Death

In the later years of her life, Elizabeth Packard continued to be a steadfast advocate for women's rights and mental health reform. Despite facing adversity and societal resistance, she remained committed to her principles, contributing to the evolving landscape of equality. As Elizabeth navigated through her later years, she witnessed the gradual shifts in societal attitudes towards women's rights. Her pioneering efforts had played a role in challenging the oppressive norms that had confined and silenced women.

Elizabeth Packard passed away on July 25th, 1897, leaving behind a legacy that extended far beyond her own life dedicated to breaking the chains of silence and oppression. Although she is no longer with us, the impact of her advocacy and the resonance of her unshackled voice endure, inspiring ongoing conversations about justice, equality and the enduring power of individual resilience. Elizabeth Packard's life remains a testament to the indomitable spirit that can spark change, even in the face of formidable challenges.

CONCLUSION

Elizabeth Packard's life was a testament to the indomitable spirit of those who dare to challenge the norms of their time. Her unwavering commitment to justice, her fierce advocacy for women's rights, and her exposure of the injustices faced by institutionalized women have left an enduring legacy.

In an era when women were silenced and confined, Elizabeth defied convention and sparked change. Her life is a reminder that even in the face of adversity, one person's determination can ripple through history, inspiring generations to stand up for their rights and for a more just and equitable world. Elizabeth Packard's legacy is one of resilience, reform, and the enduring spirit of advocacy.

Made in the USA
Columbia, SC
22 October 2025